There is No Death

OTHER BOOKS
BY BETTY BETHARDS:

Atlantis
Be Your Own Guru
The Dream Book
Relationships in the New Age of AIDS
Sex and Psychic Energy
Techniques for Health and Wholeness
Way to Awareness

Cassette tapes also available. Write for the current publication price list:
Inner Light Foundation
P.O. Box 750265
Petaluma, California 94975
(707) 765-2200

There is No Death

Betty Bethards

Inner Light Foundation • Petaluma, California

The Inner Light Foundation is a non-denominational, non-profit organization engaged in teaching, healing, research and publishing. The ILF, founded in 1969, provides on-going lectures, seminars and classes in wholistic health, spiritual awareness, interpersonal communications and other human development areas. The ILF also offers spiritual readings and teaches a basic meditation technique for self-growth and enlightenment. Betty Bethards is the founder and president.

Cover Design and Illustration: Jon Goodchild
Printed in the United States of America.

This book is lovingly dedicated to my two sons, Wayne and Chris, who taught me so much during their short time on the earth plane.

The Miracle of Life

Betty channeled this poem a short time before her eldest son was killed in Viet Nam.

Such awe is known, such love is born
    the moment your first child is born.
Such hope, such dreams you hold within
    for the tiny one's happiness and life.
The joy and love within a mother cannot
    be put into words.
How she suffers as she nurses his bumps along
    life's rocky road.
But that she could take the pain and knocks
    that life must surely give if the child
    is to grow strong and wise.

Realization comes swiftly to her when she
    understands that this child she loves and
    calls her own, is not *her* child but God's.
In his love and wisdom He lends us His child
    to love, to guide, but never to hold for long.
With love and trust she must release the child
    and let him return to God, alone.
Each must walk his own pathway back to God
    and each must be free to follow his heart.

A mother's love is strong and true
    but God's love is all embracing.
A mother may err, where God never falters.
The secret of life is growth and understanding,
    in maintaining the courage to voice your beliefs
    yet love despite the difference, to let the
    Christ-Within you shine forth so strongly that
    we then realize--Mother, Son and God are one.

CONTENTS

Go Away, You're Dead • The Beginning of Psychic Ability • First Out-of-the-Body Experience • So This Is Death • My Choice to Go Back • Understanding Dimensions • Beyond Death Through Meditation • Oldest Son Is Killed • Farewell From Grandma • A Glimpse of the Light • My Second Son Meets Death • A Beautiful Part of Life

Why Did I Live? • I'm Going Home Tomorrow • I Stopped Laughing and Started Listening • Bargaining for Time • Where's the Light? • Three Children Face Death • Grief Holds Him Back

PREFACE

Betty Bethards is widely known as a psychic, mystic, spiritual healer and meditation teacher. Her publications, lectures and media appearances have helped thousands of people find meaning in the cycles and stages of life, including the transition called death.

Betty began to realize through her own "death" experience that the *real you* never dies, but lives on in another dimension of existence. In death, she discovered, only the physical body is shed, much like shedding a worn out overcoat. Death is a beginning, not the end. It is a change in the rate of vibrations, a transition into another level of consciousness.

Thousands of people have had near death experiences, and many who have experienced a close brush with death report an overwhelming sense of peace and well-being at the moment they thought they would die. They tell of seeing loved ones who have already died and that their religious teachers are standing there to welcome and assure them. Many experienced going through a tunnel or hallway toward a brilliant light, yet they are told in that timeless state of awareness they must return to the earth plane, that their time is not yet come. And, though they are thought momentarily dead or hopeless by doctors, they suddenly regain consciousness, make a rapid recovery, and return to their daily lives.

As we consider the medical research today on thousands of death bed reports of patients, we finally may begin to gain reassurance that death is not the end. It is but a beautiful step in the ongoing process of growth and unfoldment.

In our society the inevitable event of death, which all must experience, is all too often a tabu subject. It is seldom planned for and rarely celebrated in joy. Confronting our own physical mortality, however, can be the very process that gives new meaning to life.

"After my first death experience," explains Betty, "I lost all fear of dying. I realized that life and death are part of a continuum of being. Then I began to find the real meaning of my life here on earth.

"Death is nothing more than leaving the body," she continues, "just like we do every night in the dream state. We all leave the body at night. If you jerk as you are falling asleep, it's a bad take-off. If you dream you are falling, it's a bad landing coming in. If you awaken but can't move your body, you haven't fully merged with it yet. Just take a few deep breaths, relax and you'll be fine."

Betty points out that the only difference between the death state and dream state is that the silver cord, which is an energy link much like an umbilical cord connecting the soul with the body, is severed in death. This cord allows the being to travel in the various realms and planes beyond the physical at night to receive higher teachings. In the state of so-called death, the entity severs itself from the physical body in much the same way one was severed from the mother's womb. The energy link, the silver cord, disconnects as the entity leaves the body. All knowledge gained while in the physical form is taken with you. When you leave you could care less about the physical vehicle, because you see it as a hindrance or prison.

"We fear death because we fear the unknown," Betty explains. "But we have all died many times. The problem for most of us, is that we just don't remember. Past death experiences may surface as fears about water, cave-ins, disease, fire, or however we have died.

"We are able to move beyond these fears in meditation when we realize why we chose particular methods. In the meditation state we lose all fear of death because we transcend dimensions, realizing we exist on many realms simultaneously. Only the physical body is shed when we finally check out of the earth hotel."

There Is No Death includes personal experiences of death and dying, how to understand levels of reality beyond your own, what happens when you die, and how to help others who are facing death. You learn how meditation helps prepare you for the death experience and get an inside look at other dimensions.

Most importantly, perhaps, you will begin to feel more at home in our wonderful universe. You will begin to understand why you, as an entity, can never die.

INTRODUCTION

A LETTER TO YOU

Dear Friend,

Many things in this universe we will never understand until we ourselves are allowed to experience death and see how perfect God's plan is for each of us. There is no accident or coincidence on this earth. No one can "go home" (die) until all is finished that he or she came back to do.

This book touches us at the most vulnerable and potentially life-transforming times of our lives. When we are facing our own death or the death of a loved one, we are forced to look at the meaning of life.

It often seems that nothing makes much sense. Why should a young child die? A teenager commit suicide? Why should a person die at seemingly the prime of his life? Why do some suffer and some not suffer? Is the length and quality of our lives arbitrarily determined?

Children who die young are like angels. They teach and bless everyone who has come into contact with them, and our lives are far better for the encounter. The so-called crib death always happens to an old soul, a teacher, who came in only to open our hearts to greater love and understanding of life and death. They never intended to stay in the body, but to give a great gift of love to us.

Our young people killed in "accidents" are set up by their guardian angel to be exactly where they need to be to leave the body, painlessly and quickly. If it wasn't a part of their soul's plan to go home, they would have lived. To blame anyone else, yourself most of all, for your child's death in an accident is like a festering wound that can never heal. There are lessons for those involved, or those who seemingly cause another's death. But always remember that the soul was set up beforehand to be at that exact place, at the exact time, in order to be released from the body. The soul had completed what it came back to do and God arranged all perfectly to bring the soul home painlessly. Fast death is the easiest and best karma. Here there is no need to suffer and you are released instantly. You experience no impact or pain. In an automobile accident you are out of the body at impact, watching the situation with total understanding and love. If you haven't earned your way home, you can't die in an accident. It's God's way of saying, "Sorry, you haven't earned your way home yet."

Pray for anyone you feel has caused your child's death, or the death of any friend or loved one, and know that God's laws are very just. No one ever gets away with anything. As we sow, we shall also reap. Release them with love, and know that resentment, anger and hate only hurt *us*.

Your child or loved ones on the other side hear your thoughts and words and they see what you are doing. Visualize them in your mind and talk to them. Be still and let them explain why God permitted them to go home. You will also be able to see them during the dream state as we all leave the body or earth suit at night. You can touch them, hold them and see that they are solid and alive.

If you are mourning and distraught, your energy will be too low to hear them. They want to reassure you that they are happy and well. Your suffering hurts them and holds them back from going on. They stand by us until they can make their presence felt, and then they are free to grow and learn. It's painful for them to watch us suffer when they are safe, happy and well.

The greatest gift of all is life. We need our earthsuit or body to learn how to or how not to do things. We choose our parents, our race, our culture, our sex, our time and date of birth and the lessons we want to encounter the first 28 years of our life. We all know our first 28 years when we incarnate. There are no mistakes and we choose our lessons very carefully for what we want to learn and incorporate in this life.

Life in the body is like school. Once we have learned our lessons and taught others whose lives are entwined with ours, we are free to go home. But this time here on earth is very important because it greatly accelerates our growth and understanding.

Suicide, The Big No No

When our energy gets down and we get discouraged and depressed, we may see suicide as a way to end our misery. But suicide is God's Big No-No. You set up the tests to help you grow. You have all the strength within to meet every challenge. Nothing is worth taking your life over, because you take you with you wherever you may be! There is no death! There is no escaping from yourself! A suicide will cost you from two to eight incarnations, and you will have to walk through the exact same tests you decided to take your life over.

It's your perception that says this is good--this is bad. Don't be afraid to ask for help. There are many agencies you can call, people you can talk to, people who really care.

Teenage Suicide

Teenage suicide is especially tragic. Energy is being elevated on the earth plane and as a result the veil between the third and fourth dimensions is getting thinner and thinner. This makes us more and more psychic and we're vulnerable to everyone else's mood swings.

For children, especially in puberty, the energy they experience coming into them is so intense that often they don't know how to deal with it. Many hear voices, many get depressed and withdrawn. Most have poor self-esteem and everything seems to be a struggle. The build-up of their frustration can lead to thoughts of suicide. If someone--a parent, friend or teacher--notices the signs and encourages the child to verbalize his feelings, this can often be avoided.

I hear teenagers tell me so often about their thoughts of suicide that I feel we must, as parents, teachers and counselors, help them to deal with this fast growth time.

The Prime Cop-Out

If you decide to go ahead and kill yourself, whatever your age, I consider this to be the prime cop-out. I'm angry when a friend and/or loved one take their life and I tell them off loud and clear. They have no right to lay that on those who loved them. It's the height of selfishness!

Once I tell them off, I refuse to listen to them or talk to them. Because I have such a direct line to the other side, it's easy for me to see and hear them. I tell them they didn't want to talk to me before they took their life, so now they can talk to a teacher out of the body. I send love and prayers to and for them, but I won't talk to them. I won't be manipulated by anyone in or out of the body.

Many people will threaten suicide if we don't do what they want. That's their choice and they will have to live with that choice in or out of the body. That is not my karma, nor my lesson. I can only change myself. I can't change anyone else.

Meditate and Lighten Up

The easiest way to move through life with understanding is by meditating. Meditation is the best way to calm and center ourselves so that we can look at our fears and see what we need to change in our perception of life and our purpose in the universe.

If we can lighten up on ourselves and realize we won't really know what we want to do until at least the twenty-eighth year (and maybe a long time after that), it will take some of the pressure off. Understand you are a mirror for others to see themselves in. Anything anyone is laying on you is their own stuff. It has nothing to do with you. If someone is yelling at you, they are really saying that they are hurting. Don't take it personally. When they're through yelling, ask them what they are really hurting about. We only dump on people we love and trust. If your parent, spouse or friend dumps on you, it's because they love and trust you the most. The person you dump on is the one you love and trust the most.

We're all bears when we're tired, frustrated or scared. Go outside and hug a tree or hold a hose and water your garden. Expose yourself to negative ions for twenty minutes outside and you will calm yourself right down and bring your energy up. If you are angry and reacting, ask yourself, "What am I really hurt about?" Then instead of yelling, just say, "I'm hurt or that hurt." Life is so simple when we have the eyes to see and the ears to hear.

If you're scared, sit erect, turn your palms up and mentally holler, "Help!" Take three slow deep breaths and the arms of God are instantly wrapped around you. You'll be calm and centered by the end of the third breath. Also, imagine a white light of love all around you at least a block wide. This will calm and heal you and others won't pick on you. Don't be so self-critical. You can't possibly fail in life. If you fall flat on your face, you'll simply learn how not to do it.

Dare to be you and listen only to your gut. It's the God within. We aren't walking through life alone. You have a guardian angel over your right shoulder and a team of teachers. Be still and relaxed and ask them for insight and direction. Listen for the answer! You'll get it. Listen to dreams and understand they come in symbols, so don't take them literally. Work with your dreams for problem solving.*

Know that all things must pass and time helps us see the positive lessons. They really aren't negative. If you're suffering it means you aren't loving you. Be nice to yourself and understand you become what you think. Cancel any negative thought and put in the positive immediately. You'll soon find life is a beautiful journey within yourself to untold treasures and riches.

Look Within

All answers are within you. Ask the question-- the answer will come. You've got a great team walking with you who loves you very much. Never hurt yourselves or others. Be kind to yourself and follow your gut. Then any time you face a problem, say, "Thanks, God, for this great opportunity for growth! Now what do I do with it?" Keep your sense of humor and laugh at yourself. This is all illusion. It's not reality. Humor can help get you through anything. Lifetime after lifetime, and moment after moment, it's self meeting self. Remember, you take you with you wherever you go.

You and God are a team no one can beat. Remember this. And remember that there is no death.

Good luck and happy growth.

Love,
Betty

---

*The Dream Book by Betty Bethards has over 1000 dream symbols and a guide to understanding your dreams.

CHAPTER 1:

UNDERSTANDING DEATH THROUGH PERSONAL EXPERIENCE

My first experience with death challenged all my old beliefs about the nature of reality and why we are here in the first place. I learned that if we are ever to come to terms with the meaning of our lives here on earth, we must understand the meaning of death. Only then can we see it with a total perspective, fitting all the pieces of the puzzle together. Otherwise, nothing makes much sense.

Go Away, You're Dead

My first big jolt came at 21 years old. I was married and had two children, and was devoted to my kids and bowling. I considered myself an ordinary middleclass wife and mother who enjoyed ordinary, normal things in life. But one day while I was puttering around in my kitchen, I suddenly had an intense cold chill up my spine. I looked around and saw an old friend named Jerry.

Jerry was hovering several feet above the floor. I had attended his funeral one week earlier.

"Go away, you're dead!" I screamed. But he remained, appearing to be in no hurry to leave. He was wearing the same clothes he had been dressed in at the funeral and looked just like he always had to me.

"I must be imagining things," I kept telling myself. After all, being raised a fundamentalist Baptist (later turned Methodist), I believed that when you died you were put in the ground and stayed there until Gabriel blew his horn on the final judgement day. Maybe Jerry had never learned about Gabriel, but here he was manifesting in my kitchen and I didn't want any part of it.

Jerry began communicating with me telepathically. I knew exactly what he was saying and what he wanted me to know although he never spoke a word. He told me he wouldn't leave until I agreed to write down specific details concerning the handling of his unfinished business affairs, and send them to his wife.

Reluctantly I did this, throwing in a few questions of my own to determine if this being was really Jerry, and what was going on. I felt rather silly and apologetic as I mailed the business information to his wife, who had just moved to another city. But immediately after I mailed it, Jerry disappeared and never returned.

About a week later I got back a letter: "Betty, I don't know how you did it, but you must have been in touch with Jerry. Your letter answered all my questions about handling final details. Everything checked out. And once again I feel all is well."

I then distinctly remembered events that surrounded his death. The night he died I had felt an overwhelming urge to go to the hospital in the middle of preparing dinner. My husband angrily tried to prevent me from leaving the house, but I got away and arrived just in time to be with his wife after the doctors had pronounced him dead.

I remembered my experience of going to the funeral home. I had never seen a corpse before and was afraid of the prospect. I deliberately arrived early so that I could gather myself together after viewing the body and appear strong and collected for Jerry's wife. I inched my way across the room to the casket and peered in.

Immediately I was filled with a feeling of relief. "That's not Jerry," I thought, "that's an empty shell!" All my fear left me, and I found I was looking around the room trying to find him.

As I reflected on those experiences, I realized I had been subtly prepared for my friend's abrupt visit.

The Beginning of Psychic Ability

My experience with Jerry certainly got my attention. I realized that there was a lot out there I didn't even begin to understand.

The next ten years were unsettling. I continuously had precognitive dreams about my friends and other various events, and most of the time they came true. I felt an obligation to relate some of these dreams to my closer friends, thinking that if they were aware of the possibility of hardship or danger they could avoid it. But because many of the dreams were about possible unpleasant experiences, my friends began to suggest: "Hey, Betty, do me a favor and don't dream about me tonight."

Remember, of course, that psychic phenomena and parapsychology were not in vogue in the mid 1950's and 60's, and I often wondered if I were going crazy.

During this same ten year period I went through a divorce, remarried and had two more children. I remained an avid bridge player and bowler. I also became quite addicted to working jigsaw puzzles.

The family moved often, and we were living in Bellevue, Washington, at the time of my next major spooky experience. I was 32 and was fast approaching a big crossroads in my life.

First Out-of-the-Body Experience

We all have out-of-the-body experiences, but usually we don't remember them. Every night in the dream state we are out-of-the-body, but I didn't always know about such things.

I returned home one night from a bridge game with a burning sensation in my chest and went right to bed. An hour later I awoke to find myself hovering over the bed about two feet above my body. A voice said to me, "You're going to be very sick with pneumonia. Get to a doctor."

Now this was a first. I was so frightened I reached down and pulled myself back in my body again. I had never heard of "out-of-the-body" experiences, and had no idea what was happening. Almost in tears, I awakened my husband.

26

"I was floating above my body," I cried.

"That's okay, honey," he answered sleepily, "It'll be fine in the morning."

With that consoling remark he rolled over and went right back to sleep.

But it wasn't all right. The next morning I insisted on going to a doctor. The first one assured me I was fine, to go home and take aspirin. Not satisifed, I went to an internist and asked for a chest x-ray. He looked at me with raised eyebrows, said I didn't have pneumonia, but it was my money if I wanted an x-ray. Sure enough it showed pneumonia beginning in the left lung. Again the prescription was to go home and rest. No antibiotics were given.

For the next two weeks I had temperatures of 103 to 105 degrees, and grew weaker and weaker. I began to wonder whether I was going to make it, and I felt so terrible that I wasn't sure I wanted to. At the end of this period I found myself sitting on the couch in the living room with hardly enough energy to move.

So This Is Death

Suddenly I was twenty feet across the room. Everything I considered "Betty" to be--memory, personality, senses--was looking back at that shell on the couch. I thought, "Gee, she's sick. I don't want to go back."

Then a very gentle voice said from behind me, "You don't have to go back, but this is death if you choose to stay."

27

I had a body which appeared the same, was wearing the same clothes, and was raised about two feet off the floor. I wasn't frightened at all, but felt wonderfully enveloped in peace. I knew then how Jerry had appeared to me ten years earlier. It was as if I could see things clearly, and knew that there was no such thing as death. I realized then that one never dies, but changes vibrations, and goes on living and learning on other levels.

My Choice To Go Back

I didn't really want to go back. But then I started seeing pictures of my four children flash before me. It was a tricky way to get me to make up my mind to return to the earth plane and finish what I was supposed to do. I was fine with seeing each child, knowing they could take care of themselves without me, until I saw my eighteen month old son. I knew he still needed me, and at that point I made my decision. I had to go back.

As soon as I thought this, the voice said to me again, "Unless you take an antibiotic within the next twenty-four hours, you will no longer have a choice of whether you wish to remain on the earth plane."

Immediately I found myself back in the body on the couch. As soon as my husband came home I told him I had to have an antibiotic. We found a doctor, got the medication, and the fever broke. But it took over a year for my energy level to return to normal.

It was after this experience that I knew there was no death and that it wasn't the way I had been taught to believe. I didn't know how it was, but I was determined to find out. I had to wait two years before the teachings began coming to me.

Understanding Dimensions

I realized that though we exist in the third dimensional world, by meditating we gain access to the fourth dimension.

I realized that you never die, that there is no escaping from yourself. If there is no exit from the universe, then the sobering question continues to be: why am I here and what is the meaning of my life?

My experiences in the next several years continued to be dramatic. I began to communicate telepathically with unseen teachers around me. As my energy grew stronger, old ones would leave and new ones would arrive on the scene. I perceived them as beings of light and they told me they see us as light beings, not as bodies.

They began to give me teachings I had never heard before and was hesitant to accept. They spoke of reincarnation, karma, and many other ideas that I thought were off the deep end. But I continued to listen because they were so loving and seemed so real, and I would speak as they spoke to me, recording much of the information on tape. My husband, a computer scientist, was fascinated and worked with me during many of the sessions.

These teachers identified themselves as the White Brotherhood, guardians of mankind. White means light or truth, and has nothing to do with race.

They told me that I was to be a channel of love.

The most important thing to realize is that everyone has a channel, which is really the higher self or God within. It is a level or frequency of being that we ordinarily are not tuned in to. It is what is called higher consciousness, an energy that permeates our beings and carries with it the perception of purpose, meaning, and the integration of life. It moves within and without time and space, and when we tune into it we recognize we are unlimited beings.

It is difficult to think of oneself as a composite of frequencies, of energies, when one is accustomed to thinking in terms of self as form. We like to see ourselves as male or female, young or old, and identify with certain definable limits. In order to grow beyond these limits we must learn that we have many forms, that we are energy or spirit incarnating, taking on forms through the eons.

Moving Beyond Death Through Meditation

These teachers taught me that the key to understanding the many levels of reality was meditation. Meditation heightens the energy level so that one is receptive to higher frequencies, and can consciously tune into expanded dimensions. So I began practicing a simple meditation technique they taught me, (included at the back of this book,) to refine my attunement and learn all that I could about the unseen levels of the universe that seemed to be all around me.

In the meantime I was raising my children, and

my oldest son was shipped off to Viet Nam. I was soon to face a big test: What have you really learned about the nature of death?

Oldest Son Is Killed

Wayne left for Viet Nam on October 15, 1970. That night in my meditation I asked if he would be all right and would return safely. A man's voice said to me, "Your son will be killed before March 1."

One thing I've learned in this business--don't ask if you don't really want to know. Of course I didn't want to know *that*. I totally blocked it from my mind, and imagined Wayne surrounded in the Christ light returning home safely.

That same night during meditation I was given a poem, *The Miracle of Life*, (see page VI) which was a reminder that our children are God's children and that we are all a part of the same universal energy. It also was further preparing me for his death.

In mid-January I was driving home from lecturing to a group of medical professionals. I happened to glance at a cemetary along the familiar freeway route and spontaneously said aloud, "I would never bury my son there."

A short time later that afternoon three army personnel, including a chaplain, arrived at my front door. I invited them in, but no one said anything. I finally asked, "When was Wayne killed?" He had stepped on a land mine the day before and had died instantly.

After his body was returned home, he lay in state at the mortuary the evening before he was to be cremated. I had been out to view the body twice and was getting in the car to go for a third time.

Suddenly Wayne's voice came through loud and clear. "Oh Mom, do we have to go back there again?" I flashed that everytime I went, he had to go, too.

I remembered from my own death experience that I had no empathy with my body. It was like an old coat that served me well, but I no longer had any emotional connection to it. Naturally Wayne had no use for that body and didn't care to hang-out around the mortuary. So much for my last trip.

My guidance explained that we all get to attend our own funerals, and visit until all the fuss is over. We get to know what everyone really thought of us, because we can read their minds! It's nice when someone at the service knows we can hear them and mentally talks to us. That's a beautiful gift to the loved one who has gone on.

Six weeks after Wayne's death he appeared to me in a dream. I reached out and hugged him and knew he was real. He looked just like he'd always looked in a strong and healthy body. We started having this great conversation. "What have you been doing? What are you going to do in the future?" He was telling me all about what he had been experiencing and his future plans, when suddenly I was overwhelmed with a sense of grief that my daughter Pam was dead. I woke up and began walking down the hallway, when it dawned on me. We are the ones who are dead. Those on the other side are alive.

I would dream about Wayne often, and once we had an argument over who was really dead. He said I was dead and I said he was. I began to realize what my teachers had meant when they said, "We cry at birth, and rejoice at death. It is you who are illusion and we who are reality." What we think is life is *illusion*. When others die we are really crying for ourselves, for they have earned their way home.

When we lose a loved one, particularly a child, we must deal with a tremendous sense of personal loss. It is one thing to have your own death experience and to realize that life is eternal. It is another thing to adjust to great change in our lives here on earth when another goes home before we do.

Because I felt it was important to hold together for the sake of my other children, I didn't allow myself to really mourn Wayne's death until several months later. One afternoon I went to my bedroom and had a good cry. After about 30 minutes I looked up and saw Wayne standing at the foot of the bed. He said in a rather unsympathetic voice, "If you are tired of feeling sorry for yourself now, why don't you get up and do something constructive?"

"Well, I guess that told me," I thought. I was completely out of my mourning mood.

Farewell From Grandma

In August after Wayne died my grandmother came to me in a dream. She said that she didn't always approve of the things I did when I was young, but that she wanted me to know she always really loved me. Then she said, "It's getting cold now. I have to go home. I'll have to get my coat."

When I awakened I knew immediately that she was going to die, but I didn't know when. I have learned that whenever someone says, "I am going home," they are telling you that their time of death is approaching.

I wanted to see my grandmother once more, and arranged to fly to Los Angeles to see her in September. We had a wonderful visit. In January she died, a year after Wayne's death. I then understood the meaning of "It's getting cold" and needing a coat. Her time of departure was the coming winter.

A Glimpse Of The Light

Not too long after that I went to visit an aunt in the hospital. She had been hospitalized for what she thought were ulcers, but it was actually stomach cancer. She told me that she had just had a dream she didn't understand, "Maybe you could give me some clarity. I was frightened by it, and feel that you can explain it to me."

She explained that in her dream she went into a tunnel and saw a bright light at the end of it, but that she got scared and turned around and came back.

I took her hand and said, "Honey, the next time you see that light, go for it." That's all I said, and she seemed completely satisfied with the answer. Six days later she died.

How often I have found that people are shown the pathway home before their actual time of death so they will know there is nothing to fear.

My Second Son Meets Death

My second oldest son, Chris, looked exactly like Wayne. He was 11 years his junior. Occasionally I would catch myself thinking that as Chris grew up and into his adult life, I would also get a glimpse of what Wayne might have looked like had he lived. But sometimes God seems to drive a hard bargain.

When Chris was 16 the brakes went out on his car. Time seemed to go into slow motion, and a voice said to him, "Go to the right side of the road. Keep the wheels straight." He followed instructions and was able to bring the car to a safe stop.

Later Chris said to me, "You know, Mom, I always wondered where you got your answers. Now I know. It's the same voice that talked to me and told me what to do."

This voice spoke to Chris on several more occasions when he was having trouble, including a time when he skidded on an icy road in Tahoe and was able to avoid the car rolling. He began to depend on the voice and think that he could not be hurt. But we have to remember that our guidance is there to help us in emergencies, not to be tested or set up to prove themselves. We are responsible for our own lives.

When Chris was 19 he told me he had the feeling he would die young. At 20 he had a very serious car accident. He'd worked hard all day, hadn't eaten and had one too many beers. He lost control of the car. As he was careening off the road, two 100 foot high golden pillars of light with gold light between them appeared in front of him. A voice said, "Drive between the pillars." He did, avoiding all but one small cement post. He should have been killed, but the post stopped the car and saved his life. A nurse was driving in the car behind him and called for help.

He told me later, "You know those were the gates of heaven, Mom." I knew that the next time he saw them he was going through them.

Chris was an excellent mechanic and was manager of a local service station. Soon he bought himself a motorcycle. One day I stopped by and saw the motorcycle. He said, "I know you don't approve but you might as well know it's mine."

As I looked at the bike, I thought, "So that's how you're going to kill yourself." I knew I could say nothing--he had to follow his own destiny.

One night about 8 months later I had a dream about death. I saw a calendar and then I saw a cute little fat clock with arms and legs running down the street. A man's voice said to me, "Time is running out." I woke up and looked at the time. I wrote on a piece of paper, "3:12 a.m., clock running, time is running out."

The door bell rang and I knew immediately Chris had been killed. I opened the door to find Chris's father (my ex-husband), his wife and my daughter Pam.

I said, "Chris?"

They said, "Yes."

"He's been killed?"

They said, "Yes."

He had been killed on his motorcycle as he approached the two golden pillars of the Golden Gate Bridge. He had failed to make a turn.

As I went into the kitchen to call the morgue at 3:30 a.m., I was furious. I mentally yelled, "I hope to hell you're happy! You finally did it! You and your damn motorcycle!"

Immediately Chris's voice came through loud and clear, "I'm sorry, Mom, I'm so sorry. I'm sorry, Mom."

I was *shocked* that he could come through that strongly immediately after crossing over! So I meekly said, "Well, you know how I felt about motorcycles."

Later Chris's girlfriend talked to Paul, his childhood buddy, who had been with him at the time of the accident. Paul's motorcycle was ahead of Chris. He heard him crash, looked back and saw him lying in the road, turned his bike around and raced back to him. He saw Chris jogging along beside him: "It's too late, Paul, I'm gone! I'm fine but I'm gone," said Chris. Paul just kept racing toward his friend.

Again, a nurse had been riding in the car behind Chris and was already kneeling at his side. "Don't take his helmet off," she cautioned Paul. "He has a weak erratic pulse." Taking Chris in his arms, Paul put his ear to his chest and listened for a heartbeat. The heart beat faintly five times and stopped. Again

37

he heard Chris say to him, "I told you I was gone, Paul."

The night after Chris's crossing over a group of friends got together and had a birthday celebration in his honor. It was indeed his time of new beginnings.

So two sons have gone home. That's a hard one for a heavy duty mother like me. The pain I felt was lessened by a higher understanding that life and death are two sides of the same coin. Each one of us has his or her own path and must walk that path back to God.

But there is another major consolation. I can find my children a lot easier out-of-the-body than when they were in it! When they were here I was always having to track them down! Now all I have to do is yell and they are right there!

Chris, for example, has helped me out several times. On one occasion I was in Los Angeles on my way to a radio show. The engine temperature light went on and so I pulled into a service station. The attendant explained that the radiator hose had blown and that it would take at least two hours to repair the damage because he didn't have the part. I didn't have two hours.

"Chris," I yelled, "What can I do?"

He immediately answered, "Fill the radiator with water and drive the car back to the Burbank airport and exchange it."

Now I know nothing about cars. I don't know the radiator from the engine. So I asked the attendant, "What would happen if I filled the radiator with water? Could I make it back to the Burbank airport?"

"No, but you could make it to another car rental place down the street."

"Okay, fill 'er up," I said.

I told my husband that if Chris was right on filling the radiator he would also be right on getting back to the airport. At any rate, I could always stop along the way at service stations and fill the radiator with water if I needed to. But of course, I made it all the way to the airport with no trouble, exchanged the car and got to the radio station for my show.

A Beautiful Part of Life

I have learned a great deal from my own death experience, the death of my two oldest sons, others close to me, and the many people I work with on a day to day basis. Death is a natural progression into the next level of being, and comes only when we have completed what we set out to do in any given lifetime. Our life here in time-space is a gift, because if we use it wisely we are able to grow into higher levels of understanding very rapidly.

With all this talk of the beauty of death, however, be very clear that suicide is never to be considered an option. Suicide is an attempted escape to avoid the lessons we came back to learn. Remember we have chosen to be here for a very important reason. Don't blow it by skipping out ahead of schedule.

CHAPTER 2:

UNDERSTANDING DEATH THROUGH THE LIVES OF OTHERS

Through the years I have worked with many people who have had out-of-the-body or death experiences. The stories in this chapter are representative of some of our many encounters with the other side.

Why Did I Live?

It was a typical Christmas Eve, filled with excitement and expectation. The family was looking forward to unwrapping the gifts on Christmas morning. The oldest teenage daughter was babysitting with two of her younger sisters so her mom and dad could visit some neighbors down the street.

The three year old daughter was asleep downstairs in her bedroom, and the 12 and 15 year olds were upstairs in their bedroom talking. But all at once the house was filled with flames. The Christmas tree lights had shorted and set everything on fire. The oldest daughter opened her door and saw nothing but flames. There was no way to get through to any other part of the house. She turned to her sister and said, "We've got to get out of here!"

But the 12 year old just smiled and sat down on her bed. "No, I've got to go home now." She laid down and died.

Panic-stricken, the girl looked around the room. Then an authoritative yet loving voice said to her, "Break the window and jump." She reached for a perfume bottle to throw through the window but the voice said again, "No! It like everything else in this room is hot. Break it with your hand." She did and escaped, although she was badly burned.

Only the oldest sister lived. While she was recovering in a burn center in San Francisco, one of the nurses recommended that the family call me. The girl was experiencing tremendous guilt because she had lived and the other two had died. When she later was receiving tutoring to help her catch up in school, again the tutor recommended she talk to me. A short time later the father was in the local library and pulled out a copy of one of my books "by mistake." He decided that after three such happenings they would get in touch.

The whole family came in to see me, including the other brothers and sisters. We talked about the experience and how the one who had lived need not feel guilty, because it just wasn't her time to go home. How important it is to allay guilt that so often lingers on! Her 12 year old sister had known in that moment that it was her time of death.

Your sisters got to go home because they earned it, I explained. You have other things to do in this lifetime before you will be allowed to cross-over.

It is also very important that we understand that we can picture those who have gone before us, and talk to them in our minds. They see and hear us, and we can say anything we would like to say. We can send them love, and clear up any old grievances, but we must remember that our grief only holds them back. As we release them and release ourselves, we all are free to continue on whatever plane we happen to find ourselves, to grow and learn.

I'm Going Home Tomorrow

A woman who works as an intensive care unit nurse and regularly comes to my lectures shared a very beautiful story with me. She had been taking care of a four year old boy with leukemia. One afternoon as she was getting ready to finish her shift, his little face lit up and he looked at her.

"I'm going home tomorrow. I'll be very happy, but you'll be very sad," he said.

When she came in the next day he had died.

Children often have an inner knowing and wisdom about death that adults have long since forgotten.

I Stopped Laughing and Started Listening

A brilliant engineer who lived in northern California made it a habit to disregard any reports of psychic experiences or life after death. One afternoon he had a severe heart attack and was rushed to the hospital in an ambulance. The medics could find no heartbeat, and began working on him immediately.

43

In the meantime he was having a rather extra-ordinary experience. He found himself moving through a tunnel into the light, and saw his brother sitting there in a rocking chair, smoking a cigarette.

His brother greeted him and began to recount everything the engineer had experienced in the last five years. The brother included things that absolutely no one knew about except the engineer himself.

Then the brother, relaxing in his chair, said, "You have to go back now."

But the engineer didn't want to go back. His brother insisted that he could not stay, and instantly he found himself floating on the ceiling of his hospital room.

He was watching the doctors and nurses working on him. He began to slowly merge with his body, as he heard his brother's voice explain once again, "It's not your time yet." His brother had been dead for 16 years.

When he came to, he realized that he had better stop laughing at things he didn't understand and start listening. He became a regular with the Inner Light Foundation and began practicing meditation. After seven more years, he was allowed to go home.

Bargaining For Time

A film producer in his early fifties was dying of cancer. I had given his wife a reading and was kept informed on how he was progressing. In fact several years earlier my channel had predicted that he would set up an illness if he didn't change his stress-filled lifestyle.

He had chosen to spend his remaining time at home.

One afternoon he was at home lying in bed, feeling very sick. His wife was sitting beside him. Suddenly he sat straight up. He looked at his wife and said, "Three men have come for me."

He began talking aloud to the invisible visitors. He had not yet cleared up his estate, and asked the men for 30 more days. He didn't want to die and leave his wife with a big mess to take care of. At that point he didn't even have a will.

The three agreed that he could have the 30 days, and left. During that period of time he worked as best he could to get his affairs in order. As his 30 day limit was up, he told his wife, "They are coming for me tonight, but I have to have one more week. I will ask them for one more week."

Later that evening his wife was in the other room and heard her husband talking again. She heard him say, "I need one more week." In a few minutes he called to her and explained, "They said I could have another week, but that's all the time I'll be granted."

He completed his business quickly. One week later he was sitting in a chair and turned to his wife. He explained that the three men had returned and he must go now. He died immediately.

Later his wife was relating the story to me. She explained that after that experience she had absolutely no fear of death. The mysterious "other side" has people you can talk to, even bargain with.

I thought, yes, you can bargain with them ... sometimes.

Where's The Light?

A highly respected medical specialist in San Francisco (and one of my personal physicians) decided to go for a spin on his step-son's motorcycle. He had never ridden a motorcycle before, and he was later found unconscious with the bike on top of him.

He was suffering from a severe concussion, and woke up in a hospital. He didn't remember how the accident had happened, and said he had amnesia.

(Most people who go through wrecks don't remember the trauma, because they leave the body. They call this blacking out, or amnesia. But the soul doesn't like to suffer, and it always leaves before the impact.)

The next day he was still in intensive care. His wife, an ICU nurse, was sitting beside him. He reached back to push the button to lower his bed, and began to get dizzy. The next thing he knew he was floating down a dark hallway. He felt very peaceful; happy and relaxed. "It was a beautiful feeling," he told me later.

But as he continued on, he thought to himself, "Betty says there's a light, but I don't see one. While he was looking for a light he felt something like an enormous magnet or force pulling him backwards. The next thing he knew he opened his eyes and saw a group of terrified looking doctors and nurses hovering around him. He realized he was lying on a board and had been jolted back in the body through electric shock. He had just experienced a massive coronary.

As he was later recounting his experience to his wife, he said, "You know, I have a friend who told me all about that."

My next appointment with him was some months later. When I went in for my check-up, he said, "Boy, am I glad to see you. I was just telling someone about you this morning."

He told me about his adventure, and then added that he considered it quite a gift. It had changed his whole perception of death and dying. He now realized that there was nothing unpleasant about death, but that it was very beautiful and peaceful.

For a man who often works with others facing death, it was a gift indeed. He would have found the light, by the way, if it had been his time to go.

Three Children Face Death

We assume that hospitals are well-equipped to deal with death. Surely doctors, nurses and social workers are prepared to help families move through and understand the death of a loved one. Unfortunately, this is the exception rather than the rule. Many medical professionals have no idea what death is all about and are quite uncomfortable discussing the subject. Gradually this is changing, but we are a long way from providing genuine support and guidance for those who are dying and the ones who are left behind.

I was in a hospital in San Francisco recovering from surgery. It came time for me to go home, and normally I would leap at the chance. But something told me to stay another day. When the doctor came to check me out, I told him I wasn't ready to leave yet. He was surprised, but said it was fine if I wanted another 24 hours.

The next day I was up and about when I heard screaming and crying from across the hall. The nurse walked by and closed the door, but did not go in.

She told me that a woman had just died of hepatitus and other complications from alcoholism. Her three children, the oldest only 16, were alone in the room with her. No other family members were there to comfort them and the social worker wasn't there yet. The children were terrified and started screaming and crying hysterically.

I asked if I might be allowed to go in and talk to the children because I just couldn't stand their pain. The nurses seemed grateful and hastily got me a gown, mask and gloves because of the possibility of infection from the disease.

As I walked toward the room I felt scared and prayed, "Please, God, just talk through me." I knew I had to help if I could.

I walked in and just started talking. They wouldn't look at me at first, but I just kept on going. "I want to share with you what I feel death really is," I said. "I had a death experience and will never fear death again."

As I related my personal experiences they began to grow still. After a while the oldest looked at me and said, "You know, I believe you!"

I explained that their mother could still see and hear them and that she loved them very much. She didn't want them to think she had deserted them.

The father had refused to come to the hospital. He and the mother were divorced. The children were angry that he had not come. I explained they were strong enough to handle it but that he just wasn't able to do so at the time. They could always be proud of themselves because they were there. They must forgive him, and release the mother. We left the hospital room and walked down to the waiting area. We talked for several hours.

Later the social worker came by and wanted to take the chldren back into the room with the mother to talk to them about death. I went along, and heard about pain, sadness, their mourning, how hard it would be and about as many negatives as I could stand. No wonder people have a hard time facing a death experience! Later the doctor asked me if I would stay in the room while he talked to them. I said, "After what I heard the social worker tell them, you better believe it!"

I helped them make the necessary arrangements for their mother's body and we all hugged and kissed one another before they left.

I was in such awe that I had been given the gift of

talking to those children. I wasn't allowed to check out of the hospital early because I was needed to help see them through a very special time. That experience emphasized to me just how important it is to really understand death and dying, and how inadequate words can be unless you really know what you are talking about.

Grief Holds Him Back

A 17 year old high school student had a strange dream one night. The next morning he told his mother that in the dream he and his two good friends had been riding in the family car. Another automobile came around a bend and hit them head on. His two friends were killed. He was the only one who lived.

He didn't think too much more about the dream. Two days later he was out driving in the family car with his two friends. Another vehicle came around the bend and hit them. He was the only one killed.

His mother came to me grief stricken. Why had she given him the keys to the car? What about the dream showing that he would not be killed? I explained that from the other side we are the ones who are dead. That he lived in the dream meant that he was going home, and he was now more alive than we were. But his mother was so filled with guilt and grief that she was unable to listen to me or anyone else.

Over a year later her sister dreamed of the boy, her nephew. In the dream the boy appeared to her and said, "Please tell Mom to stop grieving. She's holding me back." The sister was not into meditation or metaphysics, but she related the dream. When the mother heard it, she came back to see me.

The message was like a slap in the face to shake her out of feeling sorry for herself, she explained. She realized she had been blocking any communication with her son. That was a major turning point in her realization, and she was able to release him and to release herself.

It is so important to send positive, supportive thoughts to your loves ones who have crossed over. Your sadness and clinging simply weight them down. They can soar on your positive energy or be held back by your mourning.

CHAPTER 3:

DEATH, KARMA & REINCARNATION

Ancient Teachings About Death and Rebirth

Karma and reincarnation were hard for me to swallow at first. They were totally foreign to my fundamentalist upbringing. But as they became more and more an integral part of all the teachings I was receiving, I began to see how much sense they made. Before that I could never understand why some people were born blind, some died at a young age, some lived in wealth and others lived in poverty. The human plight just didn't seem fair. Now that I understand we create our own circumstances for very good reasons, and we have many lifetimes to live, it all seems to fit into the picture.

These interwoven concepts have been known in both eastern and western traditions since early times, and once had wide acceptance in the early Christian church. In essence they are easy to understand.

The Real You

Reincarnation suggests that a person is basically spirit or consciousness which takes bodily form, and is born lifetime after lifetime. Literally it means "spirit becoming flesh again and again." Reincarnation is a

THERE IS NO DEATH

natural, normal process of the evolution or development of the soul. The process provides the soul with the opportunity to grow and to learn until it is able gradually to raise its level of vibration so that it can enter new dimensions of being.

The soul or the etheric body is the *real you*. The soul is energy. There are layers within the soul because you have many astral bodies, or energy bodies, which you shed the higher you go spiritually. At death you shed the physical body as a coat, and emerge much as a butterfly comes forth from a caterpillar. You do the same thing on each and every level on the other side.

Sowing and Reaping

Karma refers to the law or principle which governs one's experiences over collective lifetimes and within the individual lifetime. Some people call it the cosmic law of cause and effect, and it simply means that we will harvest exactly what we have planted. As you sow, so shall you reap. It is the principle of individual responsibility: we control our own destiny by our thoughts, words and deeds.

Karma follows you from your very first incarnation and continues throughout all succeeding lives. When you build it you must pay it off. Many souls do not have to pay it off in that particular incarnation. They can wait two or three incarnations before they have to face their past ties. You can see karma working in your life today. If you hurt someone, this hurt will come back to you. If you handle situations with love, you are going to be able to conquer not only *your* karma, freeing you, but you are also going to free the other soul. It is in forgiving that you are forgiven. Each soul must be able to understand these basic laws of karma before one will truly be free from oneself: all attachments, desires, and ego identifications. As you create whatever it may be, your heaven or your hell on earth, you will constantly be meeting yourself throughout each and every incarnation.

Between incarnations one receives many teachings. When the soul returns to earth it brings back the knowledge and training and tries to put it into practical application in the body.

It is very difficult to be loving, kind, gentle and forever forgiving when you find yourself around people who are not of the same caliber. It's easy on the other side because you are only around like-minded beings, and you have much greater awareness. Many choose to incarnate when they don't really have to because it would take the equivalent of 1000 years to do out of the body what you could do on the earth plane in one short sixty to eighty year life period.

Planning Our Lives

There is an ultimate plan that God, or Universal Love, has for all creatures. Ultimately it is that they should find their way back to the infinite love power of the universe. Each individual designs a plan for his growth before each incarnation. One may receive help from teachers on the other side, but the plan is your own choice. So before each soul incarnates on the earth plane, it plans carefully what it hopes to achieve in that lifetime. It decides what strengths or weaknesses it desires to unfold or learn to control. It decides what karma it wishes to work out. It very carefully plans out the first 28 years, never to suffer but to learn how to or how not to handle something.

Everyone can know that he or she has chosen the circumstances of this present life: sex, parents, nationality, race, socio-economic conditions, astrological sign, and so on. Born out of wedlock, parents divorced, a family of alcoholics, whatever the circumstances, you have chosen them for a reason. If you are adopted, then you have chosen your adopted parents in a very closely coordinated time schedule. There are no accidents or coincidences.

The soul is still free once it incarnates to go ahead with the plan or change its mind. Your teachers, of course, are going to be there encouraging you to get on with the program. But we are free to blow an incarnation, and then we will choose to come back and do it all over again.

Why don't we remember all these great resolutions? Memory is largely erased at birth, although the spiritually developed person may see or recall his former lifetimes. Some psychics can see the previous lifetimes of others. Some people come in with such an overriding sense of what they are supposed to do that their career is never a question for them. Child prodigies are individuals with memory and skill which are carried over from other existences.

Once you understand that you intentionally selected your present existence, you are able to ask why. There is always a positive reason. If people could only realize that we have chosen our race, that we have all been many races, there would be no prejudice. People who are prejudiced must return under the same circumstances of those they condemn. We never incarnate into anything but a perfect body unless we choose it. For example, if we are born blind, we are working to develop the higher spiritual senses, deliberately cutting ourselves off from sensory input that can get in our way of listening to the intuitive. It forces us to develop the sixth sense or seeing with our inner eyes.

Most people are deaf and blind. They really can't see or hear how they are setting up their lives.

What you perceive of as suffering is actually your opportunity for growth. It is a chance to correct past mistakes and continue toward your ultimate goal. For example, if you blame your parents (or anyone else) for your unhappiness, you can be sure there is karma to be worked out. You will meet them again and again until you can feel compassion and love. In this way every relationship in every incarnation is an opportunity to grow.

Ask yourself, "Why did I choose them and what is my positive lesson?" Many times it's to learn how not to do it.

Karma and Suicide: Forget It

The greatest gift of all is life. We need our earth suit to learn how to or how not to do things. We have carefully chosen our lessons and we all have the strength within us to meet every test. We are unique and special. We have tools and treasures within that we have never before discovered.

When our energy gets down we all get depressed and discouraged. We think this feeling will never end and that life will always be agonizing. All of us reach this point at one time or another in our life and we see suicide as a way to end our misery.

Once death is understood it will immediately put an end to that idea once and for all! There is no death! We take us with us wherever we go and without this good ol' earth suit to work out our lessons in, we're going to be stuck with ourselves until we can get permission to get another earth suit, incarnate again and walk through the same thing all over until we can pass our tests.

You can't escape yourself, dead or alive. Death changes nothing because you haven't gone anywhere. You're standing there listening and watching those left behind but they can't hear you. It takes at least 80 to 120 years to come back and you usually pick up two to eight extra incarnations for suicide. Your guidance must lead you slowly back into the earth plane tests before you walk through the identical situations you took your life on. Nothing is worth that!

It's easier to say to yourself, "Since I can't die, I

may as well see how I set this mess up and get busy and love myself so I can do it right--and not have to keep coming back and doing it again and again!"

Suicide is God's Big No-No. If you jump off a bridge, you'll immediately separate from your physical body or earth suit and stand there in mid-air watching it fall. You suddenly realize you are still you. Your emotions are the same as when you jumped, and all you did was to throw away the earth suit necessary to use to know yourself.

You'll instantly see your teachers standing there looking at you and they won't be very happy with your choice. You'll wish you could turn the clock back fast and make a wiser choice, but you are stuck with your decision and your karma. We all have options and choices. Make yours wisely.

Believe me, nothing is worth taking your life over. It is the most precious gift you've got and you chose it. Ask yourself what your positive lesson was in every painful situation. You will see that nothing is negative!

Realize there is no death, that all experiences are our teachers. Don't make the costly mistake of suicide. And help others realize how precious is the gift of life!

Beyond Male and Female

A spirit or soul has no gender, is neither male nor female. When you come into bodily form, you choose the male or female body depending on what you lack. If, for example, you need to develop the tenderness and love of the mother, you would choose the female body.

We develop the intuition from the feminine parts of ourselves and the strengths and assertiveness from the masculine.

Each person has many incarnations both as a man and a woman. You need to learn to see your fellows not as male or female, but as evolving beings. See yourself the same way. You are only temporarily, for this lifetime, a man or a woman. This is not your permanent identity.

Lesbians and homosexuals lack a clear understanding of the sex role they have chosen. They are in a transitional incarnation. A homosexual may have been a woman in his last incarnation, and still feels like a woman. If he goes to all the trouble of getting a sex change operation, he may or may not find himself in a better psychological condition. He had chosen the male body for a good reason, to help him learn certain lessons, to develop certain strengths. After the operation the lessons remain the same. One should not feel guilty over a sexual preference, but should always continue to explore what the lessons are in this lifetime: Why did I choose this body? Why did I choose these circumstances?*

What About Free Will?

The will is the entity's directional force. It is the power of will which enables us to direct our lives, to

---

*These topics are more fully explored in Sex and Psychic Energy by Betty Bethards.

make choices. The will represents an individual's strength. It is the developing ability to select wisely our pathway of growth, to carry out the intent of our life plan. The will goes with one from incarnation to incarnation. It is the developing awareness of purpose, the steering mechanism that keeps us pointing forward. Will is the determination to persevere in the process of working out one's karma through numerous rebirths.

There are many arguments over whether man really has free will. From the reincarnation standpoint, we do to a large degree. We choose our pace, how rapidly or slowly we will progress. We choose our circumstances, how and when and where we will work out our karma.

We chose our actions, specific deeds, attitudes, and responses in the various relationships of life. We are always free to decide how we will respond to the situation in which we find ourselves, and that situation is itself a result of our freely chosen deeds.

Practically, there are limitations on the will rooted in the nature of physical reality. Once you choose a framework or the particular circumstances for a lifetime, you are restricted to operating within that framework. For example, if you choose to be born with a six foot brown skinned male body, you cannot suddenly decide you wish to be a petite five foot yellow skinned female. But within our framework we have all the freedom we need, and far more than we can use, for progressing in our life tasks of growth.

CHAPTER 4:

CROSS-OVER:
WHAT TO EXPECT

Not the Same for Everyone

When the soul has been exposed to the opportunities it chose for a particular lifetime, it is allowed a release from the physical body. The soul knows when the time for release has come. Death is easy — life is hard work.

Death is not the same for everyone. It depends upon how you have prepared yourself during that incarnation, how old a soul you are, how evolved your awareness, and what lessons you chose to learn through the death experience. You may have chosen to learn courage and to build strength through a physical death with suffering. People who die slow deaths from such things as cancer or strokes are often givers who have never learned how to receive. Their souls may choose a slow death in order to allow others to give to them. But you can learn your lesson and move beyond the need for pain and suffering in dying. You may, in fact, have chosen a fast and easy death. Either way it is not a punishment, but a process of growth for both you and those around you. It allows you and others to work through difficult situations with kindness and compassion.

Seeing The Invisible

When you approach the time of death, often you're able to see relatives who have crossed over standing around you. The etheric body slips easily in and out of the physical, and many times a person near death talks to beings who are invisible to others. Doctors for the most part think you are hallucinating, but you're not. Whether death comes rapidly or slowly, your loved ones know ahead of time when you are coming, and are there, prepared and waiting, happy that you have been released.

The Tunnel and The Light

First, you may experience your whole life flashing in front of you much as a drowning man reports this experience. Next, you will go through what appears to be a dark tunnel or dark tube which has a very bright light at the end. Most entities are just drawn to the light without anyone saing, "Go to the light." It's a past soul memory of having left the body many times, and knowing what to do.

This light is from higher astral levels, and you follow it to the one you have earned. However you have lived your life on the earth side determines how high you can go into the light on the other side.

There is nothing to fear. You leave your body every night as you enter the sleep state. There is no difference. You cannot be harmed.

Fears are within, and this is why you must work to release yourself from fears on the earth plane, because you will carry these same fears over to the next dimension. As above, so below!

Hanging Around

Some people may want to hang around their old surroundings on earth rather than go on to discover for themselves the beauty and wisdom which is offered to them on the other side. This may take a long time, but they are coaxed along slowly. Nothing is forced on a soul, neither attitudes nor understandings. This is why we are always counseled here on earth never to force our beliefs on another person until one is ready to hear them. The free choice of every individual should be acknowledged.

Seeing Loved Ones and Teachers

When you die you are greeted by loved ones first so that you may understand what has happened. There is a big celebration, like a birthday party, heralding your arrival. Family and friends who have gone on before you are there to celebrate your arrival.

There is always good at the time of your cross-over. Even people who have lived lives of selfishness will know and understand the rejoicing. Whatever you have sown you are going to reap in terms of structuring your experiences and lessons which continue on the other side. But the first few days of cross-over (as you know time on the earth plane) you are allowed to be with your teachers, and those who have loved you in the past. You are able to see those you left behind and to hear their thoughts and words. The first six weeks we stay very close to our loved ones on the earth plane.

You are given glimpses of things you expected to see in order to bring you comfort. You may briefly see a teacher you worshipped in your lifetime: Jesus, Buddha, or another guru, according to your expectations. After the first seventy-two hours, however, you are gently brought out of many of your illusions and shown that you have not landed in an ultimate paradise with gold paved streets. Of course you could choose to create these for yourself on this plane, but once you truly understand you would most likely choose to be around that with which you felt most comfortable.

If you don't believe in God or an afterlife, you will probably be kept in a sleep state for the first two to three day period. You will wake up in a beautiful meadow or some other calm and peaceful place where you can reconcile the transition from the death state to continuous life. You are given teachings in the hope that you do not refuse to believe that you are dead.

On the other side you see things with a clearer, more objective nature, but you are not given total knowledge because you would not understand it or be ready to use it, any more than while you are here on earth. We are given knowledge only as we are ready to receive it, whether we are in or out of the body.

After The Homecoming

After the first six weeks the soul meets with what may be called a loving board of directors. It is composed of teachers and other higher beings who have walked with you. These beings help you review your past life, to begin to look at what was learned and not learned, and what you wish to work on or do from this point. No one judges you, and this is important to keep in mind. You are the one that judges yourself and decides what is best for continued growth.

You will be given teaching, training, and anything you need to help you prepare yourself for your next incarnation. But this is not given immediately. You can choose your own pace and need not be hurried through the planes in the next dimensions. It may take centuries for your soul to know what is best for your development once you return again to a physical body. It may take a great deal of reflection before you determine a purpose and direction for your next sojourn on earth. Since we reincarnate in groups we usually wait 80 to 120 years before we come back.

Also, as part of your training, you are allowed to watch people on the earth plane to see how they handle situations when they reincarnate. Very few people in a physical body realize that their behavior is a teaching ground for those who are out of the body.

Reviewing Past Lives

As you are ready, and as you choose, you will be shown your past lives. If you do not believe in reincarnation it may take a long time before you are able to deal with this. Eventually, you must learn to understand yourself in a continuity of growth over many lifetimes. You must recognize all the strengths you have built and all the karmic ties you have created which must be dissolved.

By the time you are given the privilege of reviewing all past lives and integrating the knowledge learned, you will have reached a state of total objectivity. You will feel no remorse or condemnation, but will see it as merely a review of why situations occurred and had to be worked through.

The record of your life is very private. Only those who have walked with you as teachers are allowed to see what is called your akashic (or life) record. If during your lifetime you ask that a psychic tune into this record, he or she will only be given a minimal amount of information from it which is particularly relevant to your immediate problems or concerns.

You, too, can tune into this record through meditation and get insight and clarity on the problems you are dealing with. Your own attunement is much more accurate than asking a psychic or someone else to tell you about yourself. This builds up a dependency. We may need clarity or help at times, but should never develop a dependency on others. Our whole purpose is to gain strength and learn how to make our own decisions.

Religious Beliefs

Your religious beliefs have little to do with what you experience in the transition from one realm to another, except that you would be allowed to see briefly the teacher or guru that you followed. Regardless of cultural or religious beliefs, you will have the same basic experience at death (just as mystics of all great traditions attune to the same universal energy). What counts is what comes from the heart, not what one professes to believe. It means nothing whether or not one was baptized, for example, or whether one has various other rites administered. How ridiculous to rely on meaningless words!

The true meaning of baptism is an initiation of the spirit, an opening awareness to the God consciousness. People receive this inner baptism when they are spiritually prepared.

You will not suddenly be sitting at the feet of a man with a long white beard called God. God is within, whether you are in or out of the body. Your awareness of the God force will not be greater on the other side. If you insist upon searching for God, you will do this for awhile until you get the idea that you are following an illusion. My channel has said that we must go through at least four more planes beyond the astral before we could even begin to understand the energy of the God force. God is love in all religions, so the more we live love the closer we are to God.

Angels? Yes, such beings are there. They are entites who have gone through their own evolutionary process on a much higher level than the people of the earth plane. Each one of us is assigned one of these beings, who walks with us during life as our guardian angel. This being merely watches and records how we handle situations, arranging for us to meet those we have karmic ties with. The guardian angel loves you but remains aloof and very patient. Your teachers, however, have been on the earth plane and they influence us from birth until death.

The Idea of Purgatory. Catholics understand purgatory as a place or level of consciousness one goes for further understanding. It is an intermediary state that gives one the opportunity to develop further clarity. At first it is like being in fog, just as many people walk around on the earth plane in a fog. They don't have the clarity to understand how they are setting up their lives.

If there has been much negativity during an incarnation, or a suicide, one must spend some time contemplating what has happened.

It is a holding place where souls who are confused, who do not want to let go of their earthly attachments, or who choose not to grow will remain until such time as they allow themselves to be released to flow once more into the light.

Purgatory is a place of your own making. We see souls who are punishing themselves here on the earth plane. This continues after death just the same as it would if they were still in the physical body. Many people must suffer in order to feel worthy. When they finally learn this is a negative number they are running, they can move on.

The Meaning of Hell. What about the reality of a place called hell? Hell is a level of consciousness which can be experienced in or out of the body. It is a lonely place where one is not allowed to be in communication with anything other than one's own negativity.

Souls do not enter this level unless they need to experience it for their growth. Many people who commit suicide will have to go through this hell of their own making in order to become aware that this is not what they are striving for. The soul must learn that it does not have the right to take its own life, that it cannot kill, it cannot hurt other people; nor can it judge others for we have no knowledge what they came back to do and learn.

Many people at one time or another have experienced this plane. Alcoholics going through the DTs, people on drugs, may also see it. It is a plane of total darkness where we must confront the fears we have built within our own minds. Understand that fears have no reality unless we choose to give them reality. As soon as we are able to meet them directly, to face them, they dissipate. This lower level is not for one's punishment, but rather to provide the opportunity to confront and move beyond the negativity created by oneself.

The hell fire mentioned in many traditions is symbolic of the kundalini energy (Holy Spirit, God energy, or Creative energy) that dwells within the seven energy centers or chakras within man. Fire is symbolic of the cleansing and purification of the soul.

The struggle between higher and lower self or what some call God and the Devil causes growth, until finally the negativity or the destructive elements are completely overcome.

CHAPTER 5:

SOCIETY ON THE OTHER SIDE

Laws More Protective

Through questions and answers I have received information about what it is actually like to be on the other side. First, my channel has pointed out that the laws are much more protective. We need no longer be exposed to both good and evil, for we have already experienced that. We see the bad only if we choose to. Those who are living in harmony will not be imposed upon by the ignorant, but can visit the lower planes to help another if they choose to do so.

For example, if you loved someone who is on a lower vibration than you are, you are allowed to visit anytime you choose by simply lowering your rate of vibration. This may help the entity greatly by encouraging self-love and growth. However, the entity will need to incarnate again on the earth plane to test out these new lessons, because it is the earth experience that determines your stage of evolution.

Freedom to Create What You Want

Once you cross over you may choose to do whatever you wish. You may lie in the sun all day, go fishing, whatever interests you. Many people realize they had not taken the time to develop their creative aspects while on the earth plane, due to many karmic ties which had to be worked out. They, then, will take the time to do some of these creative things.

People who are writers will continue to write, those who love music will continue to be involved in music, and so on. There are enormous libraries, universities, all types of creative outlets and sources of information. The soul can learn anything it chooses to learn. All one has to have is the desire to learn and the belief that you can accomplish this. Life does not stop when you cross over: it begins.

Whatever you can imagine, you can create, because all is built through the imagination. Lovely homes, beautiful gardens, snow-capped peaks, every kind of environment you would want is available to you. The color and sound are far more beautiful on the astral than on the earth plane because they are higher and purer frequencies. On the earth plane you create through your imagination, but it takes awhile to manifest because you are living within time and space. On the other side what you imagine manifests instantly. It is important to work on increasing your creative side while on earth, because what you are imagining you are creating not only on the earth plane but in the realms beyond.

You may manifest whatever is pleasing to you, whatever you are comfortable with. You may create country cottages, banquets, jewels, whatever you desire. There is no condemnation for wanting those things or images. Eventually, you will elevate your consciousness above the astral realm and these images will seem less important. You will find that you lose much of your desire for them. But as long as they bring you pleasure and you enjoy them, you are welcome to them.

Marriage and Unions

There are unions of souls on the other side, and marriage as such is optional. If couples prefer to remain together they may do so, as long as their interests and growth are taking them in the same direction. If they choose to go in different directions, there are no hurt feelings. There is no possessiveness or demands. You are free to go your own way, in your own time, at your own choosing.

Married couples will be reunited after death, and may choose to stay together if they want to, provided they are on the same level of vibration. This is free will. If you have been married three or four times, you will find that you will want to be with the one whom you truly love. It could even be someone from another incarnation. You will be with those you love, and there is a total merger which is a much higher experience and a deeper love bond than anything which you can know on the earth plane.

This total merger is like stepping inside of one another's auras, a total blending of energies. It's a way of expressing love and sharing. What you know on earth as a sexual relationship takes the form of a higher merger of souls. There is no need for sexual organs on the other side unless you choose to have them. For this merger of energies is far superior to the physical mechanics of the sexual experience. This merger is not limited to husbands and wives, but may be experienced by any two souls who are loving and caring.

Communication With Others

Just as we learn to communicate through telepathy here on the earth plane with other people as we develop our awareness, so we communicate on the other side. There is a common telepathic communication among all souls. All languages are instantly translated into what the individuals speak and understand. There is no language barrier, for you understand everything that is related to you. Your thoughts and the thoughts of others consequently are heard on every realm and every level. It takes only a few days to learn the ease in communicating telepathically when you first cross over. This leads to a great deal of growth on the part of the soul, for one is truly learning communication after death. You will know everyone's thoughts, views, and feelings like you were never allowed to know in the physical vehicle.

You can tune into anyone around you like dialing a radio station. But most souls, after the first few days of listening to the thoughts of others, get bored and go on to other things. It would be like you had 200 people in one room, and you could hear their thoughts, their ups and downs, night and day. You would soon grow weary of listening to their disharmonies.

People radiate a light which shows where they are coming from, and others know simply by looking at the aura. Nothing is hidden. Everyone is in this same level of communication. It is not a threatening, but an enlightening experience.

Understanding Realms Beyond The Earth Plane

My channel has explained that there are seven planes, and within each are seven more levels. People may basically look alike, operating in similar physical vehicles, but each person is manifesting at a different rate of vibration depending upon one's evolution. This is why some people are more spiritually advanced and others more material. People of a similar evolution tend to mingle here on the earth plane.

Each plane is a vibratory rate. We may ask: where are these planes? But we have to remember that we cannot grasp the idea of higher dimensions by thinking in terms of time and space as we know it.

The planes are right where we are now, inherent within the soul. All higher planes are within and around you, intermingled with the earth plane. You experience the level to which you have learned to attune your consciousness. When you have learned the lessons of a particular vibration, such as learning the lessons of the earth vibration, you may move on to a finer vibration of experience.

When you die you don't go anywhere, no homes in the sky. You are instantly in the fourth dimenson. Remember that heaven is not a place. It is a state of being, an attunement. It is dependent upon self, for self makes its own heaven or hell.

Beings who have crossed over are living at a different rate of vibration right where we are now. You could have a church sitting on top of your house and you wouldn't know it. A train could run through your living room and you wouldn't see it. Only as you raise your vibrations are you going to be able to see life around you as it exists in other realms. And this happens through raising the energy level of the etheric body through meditation.

My channel has named only the next two planes: the one immediately beyond the earth is the astral, and the next highest is the celestial. A soul goes to the celestial only after it has gained that perfect balance within itself and has completed all earthly karma. And from that level no one has to incarnate again.

But, you can always choose to return for a life of service. Then you go back, putting on your astral coat and physical body, to work with mankind. Once you enter the earthly realms, however, you are open for karma. If you create any it must be worked out immediately as you will have no other life in which to do it.

The majority of people presently on the earth plane will reincarnate although there are some who can complete their earthly karma in the present incarnation. It is through self-discipline, prayer, meditation and patience. We must align ourselves to higher vibrations. We are always free to choose whether to control the emotions or let the emotions control us. And this is the key: emotional control, plus total balance physically, mentally and spiritually.

Life And Death Cycles On The Other Planes

Once you have completed going through the death cycles of the earth plane, you never again go through one. As you advance to the higher planes you experience rather an initiation which takes place to shed the outer layer (as when you shed the physical body). The heavier matter which makes up your coat for one level is shed for a lighter coat when you move to the next. You shed your old beliefs and lessons and attune to your new body, a little like a snake shedding its skin. (People who are meditating are constantly lightening their bodies in order to receive higher and higher teachings. You cannot reach knowledge which is beyond your rate of vibration without raising your consciousness to that point.)

These planes extend throughout the universes. There are other universes which we do not know of intermingled with ours at a different rate of vibration. Millions of planets throughout the cosmos have life and death cycles equivalent to our earth plane life cycles. There are a few universes which have planets identical to earth. But within our own universe, there is no other planet with the same rate of vibration with people who look as we do. The inhabitants are a different frequency, a different rate of energy. Some of these beings have been sighted, and are often described as having a blue light emanating from them. This is because they are lighter than physical matter and more light shines through.

There are special vibrations associated with each planet, and each level within each planet. We go back to various planets in between earth incarnations to study. Our choice of realms and places is dependent, again, upon our level of perception and what we are learning.

CHAPTER 6:

PREPARING OURSELVES AND OTHERS

Teaching Our Children

Most of our responses toward death are learned. Children have little sense of death because they are so closely attuned to the intuitive side of their nature. They know only life, and cannot conceive of themselves as not existing. Parents, for the most part, do not think children can understand death and so they do not answer their questions honestly, or cannot because they themselves don't know.

Recently I counseled with a mother and her five year old daughter about the death of the husband. The child asked me many questions, such as, "Why did God take my Daddy away?" "Is God punishing us by taking Daddy?" All these feelings are there and should be dealt with openly. I told her that her Daddy was still with her, and that it had just been his time to go home. He had finished what he was supposed to do on earth for this life.

She said, "I know he's all right because I talk to him." Children, much more so than adults, can often see and communicate with those who have crossed over. They should be encouraged in their understanding of continuous life from their very first experience with a physical death, whether it may be an animal, friend, or family member.

A very sad situation developing today is that of teenage suicides. This represents a total misunderstanding of the whole life process. Young people who have everything to live for are too baffled by the pressures around them, and those who might offer a listening ear often do not think that teenage problems are important. It is helpful for us to remember that questions we ask and problems we deal with at every age are important, and that each step along the way lays the foundation for either future confidence or confusion.

Self-Awareness, The First Step

But how are we to offer help to our fellows if we have not been honest and open with ourselves, endeavoring to look at and move beyond our own fears and limited understanding?

As we get older the fear of death is often really a fear of life. We are too afraid to live our daily lives, and so we have this haunting feeling that there is something we're supposed to be doing, getting on with the program, and we aren't doing it. When one feels that life has been lived to the fullest there is no remorse at the time of physical death.

This is a time when we must be involved with our own self-awareness so that we may reach out and help those around us. The world today needs a lot of help! Overcoming the fear of death changes our whole perspective on life. Everything we do and think and feel takes on new meaning. When we realize that we are not limited by the physical, we begin to get the idea that we are really master of our own destinies and we more fully align ourselves with the eternal nature of our beings.

Sometimes people are given a close brush with death in order to reroute them into a more positive state, making them more aware of the special role they have chosen to fulfill in this incarnation. Those who have death experiences, who medically die and then return to their bodies, have been given this experience in order to bring about a drastic change in their way of thinking. In many cases their life beforehand was being wasted, and afterwards they work to help others in a life of service.

Getting A Perspective

There are several things to remember that are very important in getting a wider perspective on death: the departed entity's feelings toward the funeral; loved ones and the grieving process; how we can overcome the energy loss when a loved one dies; how we can rid the self of hurts or guilts which weren't resolved before another crossed over.

First, as I mentioned earlier, every one of us is allowed to attend our own funeral. If you ever wondered what cousin John really thought of you, you will have your opportunity to find out. You get to see and hear the thoughts of all present, whether they really thought you were a great person or a jerk. Also, you will feel absolutely no identification with the physical body, and certainly not with a strange graveyard you may happen to be stuck in. Yet every time someone in your family journeys out to put flowers on your grave, you will be pulled back to be there.

Choice of Cremation

It is actually better for the deceased to be cremated, because it has a more complete psychologically releasing effect both on those who remain on the earth plane and on the entity.

My channel explained, *The soul usually will prefer a cremation to a burial. Burial causes people to go out to the cemetary and grieve. With cremation and scattering of ashes it is easier for the soul who has entered the so-called death state. It then does not have to keep going to the graveyard which it has to do if people are grieving there. Every time people go to view the grave or to put flowers on it, the soul must go, and the soul really can't relate to that body in the ground. The soul has used it, the body has fulfilled its purpose, but now it has no meaning whatsoever. The soul sees no reason to set up a tribute to that body which has nothing to do with the real being anyway.*

The Process of Grieving

It is normal to grieve over the loss of a loved one, but we should remember that the pain is our sense of loss and has nothing to do with the state of the entity who has crossed over. The entity is experiencing a joyous reunion, and we are feeling sorrow at losing physical contact with the entity.

If we can understand that there is a perfect time and place for each of us to leave the earth plane, and that the being who has gone has completed his or her tasks for the lifetime, then our period of crying should be greatly lessened. Your thoughts of grief and sadness, if continued, will pull the entity back to the earth vibration when it really has much better things to be doing. We should really focus on sending love energy and support, a sense of excitement and well-being, to the one who has departed. This energy of love and joy will help propel the soul into its new experience in the higher realms.

Losing An Infant

Also, when an infant dies it is primarily a lesson for those around the infant. It always means that the child is a very old soul, bringing the parents a special lesson about the love of God. Many incarnate just as teachers. They have come in only to teach parents and others who are close to them. Many times it saves marriages. It forces us to reach out for support and love. We look for life's purpose and it opens new depths in us we didn't know existed. They are gifts and they choose us to teach so hopefully we'll see our relation to God in both life and death. When the very young die it means that they have finished their work on the earth and should not be forced to stay around. We can leave as soon as we have done what we set for ourselves.

Releasing Those Who Are Approaching Death

We should consciously tell our loved ones that we are releasing them, sending them on with Godspeed. Often a person will hang on to the physical body, postponing the actual time of physical death, because someone in the family refuses to mentally release the person. We must realize that death is a continuing process of growth and that we should not stand in the way of another's development. We should always put the person in God's hands, releasing the soul mentally to God's perfect plan.

After hearing one of my lectures on death, a physician went to the bedside of his mother who was dying of cancer. She had been holding on and experiencing a great deal of pain. He had not been willing for her to die. He took his mother's hand and said that he understood now, and that it was all right for her to go home. He assured her of his love. That night she died quietly, free from pain.

Clearing Up Old Guilts And Grudges

To be completely free from karmic attachment you must release yourself and others, whether they are in or out of the body. Often when a person crosses over we feel there is something left unsaid or undone. We feel guilty, hurt, angry, or still involved in a negative way with the entity. At this point you should practice forgiving, releasing and moving on. You can always clear karma with another whether in or out of the body, by picturing the person in your mind and talking together. Remember that they *hear* and *see* you. Imagine that you are thanking one another for all you learned together. Remind each other that all the experiences you shared were jointly created to promote growth and insight. Then send one another love and affirm that each releases himself and the other to love, learning and continuous growth. Remember if you harbor negative feelings toward yourself or others, whether in or out of the body, you will limit your awareness and retard your growth. You will also have to incarnate with them again to work it out.

When You Lose An Energy Link

When a member of a couple dies, especially if they are old, often the other partner will follow within a year. This happens because the polarity of energy between them has been broken, and one member is taking that energy link which fed the other. If a couple has grown old together without establishing close outside friendships, activities, or other things from which they draw energy, then one will usually die shortly after the other. If they have been meditating over a period of years then they would have established their energy link with the love force, and would easily sustain themselves independently.

Remember that even a healthy person may suffer when he loses the loved one he was depending upon for energy. It is important to stay active, be around positive people, get involved in projects that help continue your growth. Working with children is especially helpful, because you not only are able to help them, but are revitalized by their energy fields. Sometimes when people grow old there may be five to ten years when they have a choice of whether to continue on or leave. One can cause the body to die sooner with depression and discontent. We have an obligation to live, and should make the most of our time in the body. But even if you are working to rebuild your energy, remember that it may take about a year to return to your normal energy level after a close loved one crosses over.

Special Visits
By choice entities may return to be with loved ones and relatives on earth in times of crises or on special occasions, such as holidays and celebrations. Also, they may appear to you and communicate with you in your dream state, or you may sense their presence during a meditation period. This simply reinforces that they haven't really gone anywhere, and that we are all a part of the same universal energy.

Symbolic Meaning of Religious Teachings
The prophets of old and all truly great religious teachers tried to help people realize that death does not exist, that it is merely a transition or rebirth. They tried to explain symbolically that man dies only once within the self, and that this death is the death of the lower self going into God consciousness. The death or relinquishing of a limited consciousness is not understood, for the most part, and people fear the

natural transition from one state to another. It means nothing more than continuing growth.

Many of the original translations of the various world scriptures which were very clear on the meaning of continuing life have been lost. Jesus, Buddha, and other great sages talked of the continuation of life, but many of these teachings were misunderstood. It is because this truth has been hidden from most of us that we are not free from the fear of the unknown.

Although popular level religions have talked about heavens and wonderful rewards in the afterlife, the sadness and somber ceremonies surrounding funerals have created fear, guilt, and misunderstanding in people's minds. People often have horrible ideas about death which they suppress, never accepting the fact that one day they, too, must die.

Death as Regeneration

Death as a process of regeneration is an ancient theme. Traditions of old taught one how to die, the stages one goes through, and how to maintain awareness and experience the process fully. It is only because we have separated ourselves from an awareness of our true spiritual nature that the idea of death sounds grim and foreboding.

If we meditate daily, by the time we are ready to shed our physical bodies the process of changing vibrations and entering expanded levels of consciousness will be old hat. It will be something we can look forward to after a job well done on the earth. We can participate fully in the experience. It is too beautiful an experience to miss through fear or ignorance!

To see death in its beauty is also to realize the beauty of life on earth. It is a great privilege to be allowed to incarnate, because we have the opportunity to learn so much so quickly. No state of awareness is permanent, and we are constantly changing the way we choose to express cosmic energy, which is the ground of our beings. We move from one form to another, one manifestation to another. Eventually we merge our consciousness with the formless, the God energy, which manifests through all life expressions, all forms.

My channel has given me many teachings on the nature of death. The following is a composite of several trances. If we could but live these truths, our lives would be transformed here on earth.

The Nature of Death

Life is eternal. There is no *death*. If people correctly understood death, they would no longer have any fear of the unknown. Death is but an inevitable transition that each soul makes when it leaves the physical body. It is a freer state which does not limit the soul to time and place.

Death is a change in the rate of vibration. The energy force or soul which is the real you sheds the lower vibration of the physical body at death. The body returns to dust, because the etheric or energy body no longer resides within the physical vehicle. In the state of so-called death, the energy, your spirit, leaves the physical body and does not return. Your personality, memory, everything you consider to be you will leave with this energy because you are energy.

What we think of as *life* and *death* are merely transitions, changes, in the rate of vibration in a continual process of growth and unfoldment. The Life energy, God, underlies all experiences of life and death and is the Changeless. We will never be free from the cycles of death and rebirth until we come to know this Energy behind all appearances, all cycles, all stages of growth. When we know the One, the ground of our true being, we begin to identify with our eternal nature, rather than the stages we are going through at any particular moment in any particular lifetime. To know the Self is to know all things.

APPENDIX

INNER LIGHT FOUNDATION
MEDITATION TECHNIQUE

The underlying teaching of the Foundation is meditation, for it is through your daily practice of meditation that you open your world of inner awareness, and achieve harmony and balance in your life. All you need are a few simple tools to attune to the Teacher within you. You are your own Guru.

The Inner Light Foundation method of meditation is simple but powerful. Meditation is a deep relaxation of body, mind and spirit. It should be done on a daily basis for twenty minutes at whatever time best suits your schedule. The easiest way to meditate is to listen to your favorite songs and music. While sitting with your spine erect, you are aligning to the God Force.

1. Sit in a chair with your spine erect, shoulders relaxed, feet flat on the floor. Fold your hands together in your lap and close your eyes.

2. Take three slow, deep breaths, exhaling to the base of your spine, and feel yourself relaxing. Sit with your hands together for ten minutes.

3. After ten minutes, open your hands, palms up, laying them gently in your lap. Keep your focus on the songs and the music.

4. At the end of this ten minute period, when your energy is at its highest, most centered point, you can do your affirmations and visualizations, such as "The perfect career is manifesting in my life now," or whatever you are choosing to create in your life, i.e., wisdom, clarity, prosperity. If your buttons were jammed during the day, you can review the situation, see what your positive lesson was, and visualize how you would have liked to have handled it. This way, next time it comes up, as it will until the lesson is learned, you will handle it with love.

5. After completing your affirmations and visualizations, close your hands into a fist and feel a balloon of white light one block around you so that you're in the center. This sends love and healing out to the masses and buffers all negativity from coming in to you.

This twenty minute period, however, is not our only meditation practice. We endeavor to practice the meditation attitude, watching our thoughts and behavior, throughout each day. Meditation will also help you get a recall on your dreams. It is your greatest free tool for self-growth and self-understanding. Meditation can thus help us to be more fully involved in life because we can watch how we set up our experiences. Sometimes changes are subtle and sometimes dramatic. Meditation does change your life because it changes you.